I0426976

Table Of Contents

DON'T SHUT THE F$CK UP!
Transform Your Selling Mindset!

Introduction

Welcome to a journey of real insights into the art of selling. With over 35 years of diverse sales experience, I've encountered every imaginable product and service. My client list includes Toyota Motors, Cedars Sinai Hospital, Los Angeles Dodgers, Disney Corp, Warner Bros, Museum of Contemporary Art, Universal Studios, Los Angeles Convention Center, Honda Center, Tao Restaurant Group, MGM, BOKA Restaurant Group, Patina Restaurant Group, just to name a few. My initial training provided some effective methods, but it also exposed me to outdated and ineffective approaches. Through trial, error, and reflection after each interaction, I unearthed hidden factors that significantly impact the sales process.

I rejected the stereotypical "salespersony" tactics, realizing the importance of genuine connections over the traditional salesperson image. Basic interpersonal dynamics, often overlooked in conventional training, emerged as game-changers for me. By understanding and leveraging these dynamics, I successfully separated myself from the crowd, fostering sales relationships that resulted in a remarkable 90% sales success rate.

Central to this success were 15 mental questions that became the key to simplifying the sales process and determining the viability of a sale. This transformative approach not only made sales easier but also had a profound impact on my personal relationships and self-awareness.

In challenging traditional sales advice, such as the outdated "Shut up the F*ck up and Listen" I have learned to "Don't shut the f$ck up" and use these techniques to start creating relationship's instantly and get hired by the prospect I am trying to sell. In today's post-pandemic sales landscape, where face-to-face interactions are diminishing, making the most of every live conversation is crucial. The provided 15 questions and answers are designed to equip you with the mental tools to comprehend the intricacies of the sales process. Turn your prospects into willing listeners and collaborators, rather than adversaries perceiving you as a conventional salesperson. Join me in this exploration, and by the end, you'll possess the skills to not only succeed in sales but also enhance your personal and professional relationships.

These Self Motivating Questions will change your perception of the sales process and give you the ability to sell anything to anyone!

Question 1: Do you know who is in charge?

YOU ARE IN CHARGE!!

In the world of sales, the question always arises: Do you know who is in charge? This usually involves trying to find a decision maker and it completely loses the REAL dynamic mind shift necessary for becoming successful in sales! YOU ARE IN CHARGE! While they may need the product or service, you have the power to guide the process or shut it down completely. Embrace your role as being in charge of your product or service and take control of the process. You want to sell them and they want to buy but you need to feel strength in your side of the relationship. This chapter delves into the importance of recognizing and embracing your own authority in a sales interaction, explaining how it can shape the trajectory of the entire sales relationship process.

Understanding Your Authority:

In the realm of sales, recognizing your own authority is akin to wielding a powerful tool. While customers may be seeking your product or service, acknowledging that you hold the reins in guiding the process is fundamental. It's not about asserting dominance, but rather understanding the influence you possess in steering the interaction.

Guiding or Halting the Process:

Your authority grants you the ability to guide the process with finesse. You can shape the conversation, address concerns, and highlight the unique value of your offering. However, it also gives you the power to shut down the process if necessary. If a potential client is not aligned with your product or service, recognizing your authority allows you to make a decisive choice – continue with the sale or gracefully disengage.

Examples of Embracing Authority:

Consider a scenario where a customer is unsure about a particular feature of a product. In a conventional sales approach, the customer's uncertainty might lead to hesitancy, potentially affecting the sale. However, by recognizing your own authority, you can proactively address their concerns, providing additional information, and guiding them toward a confident decision.

Imagine a situation where a customer is indecisive about the pricing structure. Rather than waiting for them to make the final decision, you, as someone in charge, can present flexible pricing options, showcasing your commitment to finding the best solution for their budget.

In a B2B setting, knowing who is in charge can involve understanding the dynamics of the customer's decision-making team. By recognizing your own authority, you can navigate the complexities of dealing with multiple stakeholders, ensuring that your expertise is utilized in guiding the collective decision.

A customer raises concerns about the pricing of your service. Understanding your authority enables you to address these concerns with confidence. You can articulate the value proposition, explain the investment benefits, and guide them toward understanding the long-term advantages, reinforcing your position as the trusted advisor in the interaction.

Graceful Disengagement:

There may be instances where your product or service is not the right fit for the customer. Recognizing your authority allows you to gracefully disengage, sparing both parties from pursuing a mismatched partnership. This not only preserves your time and resources but also upholds your integrity and reputation.

Embracing the Role:

Embracing your role as being in charge of your product or service is not about exerting control for the sake of dominance. It's about realizing the responsibility and influence you have in guiding the sales journey. This shift in perspective empowers you to approach the interaction with confidence, conviction, and a keen awareness of your own expertise.

Balancing Strength in the Relationship:

While the ultimate goal is to make a sale, recognizing your authority ensures a balanced relationship. Yes, you want to sell, and they want to buy, but the strength on your side of the relationship is pivotal. It's about maintaining a healthy equilibrium where both parties contribute to the exchange. This recognition of authority fosters mutual respect and sets the foundation for a successful and collaborative partnership.

Conclusion:

In conclusion, understanding and embracing your authority in a sales interaction is a strategic must. This chapter has explored the dynamics of being in charge – guiding the process, addressing concerns, and even knowing when to gracefully step back. By recognizing your influence, you not only navigate the sales journey effectively but also cultivate relationships built on trust, integrity, and mutual understanding.

Question 2: Does your company actually want this customer?

In the dynamic world of sales, where the primary focus is often on securing transactions and expanding the customer base, there's a question that's frequently overlooked but holds substantial importance: Does your company actually want this customer? This question introduces a nuanced perspective that goes beyond the immediate sale, urging businesses to consider the long-term impact and strategic alignment with their goals.

Strategic Assessment:

The provided answer encourages a strategic assessment of the customer's fit within the broader goals of the company. It prompts businesses to look beyond the urgency of making a sale and to consider whether the potential customer aligns with the long-term vision and objectives. This shift in perspective emphasizes the importance of strategic decision-making in sales.

Anticipating Challenges:

Not every customer is the right fit, and being selective is crucial for sustained success. This involves looking beyond the immediate benefits of a sale and considering factors that could pose challenges in the future. Examples cited, such as the possibility of default or difficult interactions, highlight the multifaceted nature of customer relationships.

Learning from Past Examples:

We all know the "Bud Light situation" and it underscores the idea that businesses can learn valuable lessons from past experiences. It's a reminder that the selling environment is complex, and the consequences of engaging with certain customers can have lasting effects. By reflecting on past examples, companies can refine their approach to customer acquisition, steering clear of situations that may have negative repercussions.

Navigating Complications:

The acknowledgment that the selling environment is getting increasingly complicated resonates with the evolving dynamics of consumer behavior, market trends, and external factors. Answering the question of whether your company actually wants a particular customer requires navigating these complications. It involves a keen understanding of potential pitfalls and challenges that may arise during and after the sales process.

Selective Decision-Making:

The overarching message is clear: not every customer is a good fit. It's a call for selective decision-making, recognizing that the benefits of a sale must be weighed against the potential drawbacks. This strategic approach aligns with the broader concept of customer relationship management, emphasizing the quality of relationships over sheer quantity.

Aligning with Long-Term Goals:

A key aspect brought to the forefront is the importance of aligning with long-term goals. While an immediate sale might be tempting, assessing whether the customer fits into the overarching business strategy is paramount. This consideration involves evaluating the customer's potential impact on the company's reputation, relationships with other clients, and overall trajectory.

Conclusion:

In conclusion, the question of whether your company actually wants a particular customer injects a crucial element of strategy and foresight into the realm of sales. It's a reminder that successful sales aren't just about acquiring customers; they're about building sustainable relationships that contribute positively to the company's long-term objectives. By assessing potential challenges, learning from past examples, and navigating the complications of the selling environment, businesses can make informed decisions that lead to lasting success. Ultimately, this question prompts businesses to think beyond the immediate sale and consider the enduring impact of their customer relationships.

Question 3: Can this customer actually buy your product or service?

In the complex landscape of sales, the often-overlooked question of whether a customer can actually buy your product or service is a critical determinant of the efficiency and success of your sales approach. This question goes beyond mere interest and delves into the practical aspects of logistics, qualification, and the potential for a fruitful engagement.

Considering Practicality:

You need to evaluate the customer's capability and qualification. It's not just about their interest or enthusiasm but about practical considerations. Can this customer realistically make a purchase? This involves a comprehensive assessment of various factors, from their financial capability to logistical considerations.

Preventing Wasted Effort:

In the fast-paced world of sales, where time is often of the essence, investing resources in prospects who might not qualify or genuinely benefit can be detrimental. Not every potential customer may be a suitable fit for what you offer, and it's crucial to assess whether their needs and expectations align with what your business provides. This step is not just about closing a deal but about ensuring a mutually beneficial relationship.This question acts as a filter, allowing sales teams to focus on leads with higher conversion potential.

Logistics and Delivery:

The answer wisely expands the scope to include logistics—can you deliver to them? In the age of global commerce, this consideration is paramount. Beyond the ability to pay, ensuring that your product or service can physically reach the customer is vital. This logistics-oriented perspective adds a layer of practicality to the sales process, preventing potential barriers that might hinder a successful transaction.

Strategic Decision-Making:

The overarching message is clear: don't waste time on prospects who might not qualify or genuinely benefit. This advice aligns with strategic decision-making in sales. While the temptation might be to pursue every potential lead, the reality is that a more targeted and discerning approach can yield better results. This question prompts sales teams to be selective and focus their efforts where there is a higher probability of success.

Qualification for Mutual Benefit:

The idea of qualification is not solely about the customer meeting certain criteria; it's also about mutual benefit. A qualified customer, in this context, is someone whose needs align with what your product or service can fulfill. This nuanced perspective elevates the sales process from a transactional exchange to a strategic partnership where both parties stand to gain.

Deepening the Sales Relationship:

By asking whether the customer can actually buy your product or service, you're not just assessing their financial capacity; you're delving into the potential for a deeper sales relationship. It's an acknowledgment that successful sales go beyond a one-time transaction; they involve understanding, qualification, and the establishment of a connection that extends beyond the point of purchase.

Conclusion:

The question of whether a customer can actually buy your product or service is pivotal in navigating the intricate terrain of sales. It transcends interest and delves into the practical aspects of qualification, logistics, and mutual benefit. By evaluating these factors, you can optimize your sales approach, focus on leads with higher conversion potential and build relationships that extend beyond a single transaction. In a world where time and resources are valuable commodities, strategic decision-making in response to this question can be a game-changer in the pursuit of sales success.

Question 4: Are you excited at what you are capable of doing for them?

The emphasis here goes beyond merely selling a product or service; it's about demonstrating what you, as an individual can personally do to help the customer! It's about showcasing your personalized value and transforming a transactional encounter into the inception of a genuine, mutually beneficial relationship. This chapter delves into the significance of expressing enthusiasm for the impact you can personally make for the customer, going beyond the conventional boundaries of the product or service.

Embracing the Opportunity:

As the sales process evolves, the focus transitions from merely qualifying the customer to building a tangible relationship. At this juncture, seize the opportunity to convey your genuine excitement about what you can personally bring to the table. This excitement arises from the assurance that you've identified a qualified customer with genuine potential, eliminating the risk of wasted time on both ends.

Examples of Personalized Value:

Consider practical examples like offering free shipping, providing complimentary samples, or extending exclusive discounts. These tangible gestures not only showcase your commitment to customer satisfaction but also embody the shift from a transactional mindset to a personalized, customer-centric approach. It's about adding a human touch to the interaction, distinguishing you from others in the market.

For instance, imagine you're selling skincare products. Expressing your excitement could involve offering personalized skincare routines, complimentary samples tailored to their skin type, or exclusive discounts on products they've shown interest in. These personalized touches go beyond the standard transaction, demonstrating a genuine investment in the customer's well-being.

The Essence of Relationship-Building:

The provided examples, such as free shipping or discounts, serve as tangible examples of your commitment. It's not merely about the company's offerings; it's about your personal dedication to ensuring the customer's needs are met. This distinction becomes pivotal in establishing trust and rapport, essential elements in the foundation of a long-lasting relationship.

Moreover, this stage in the sales process is an opportunity to position yourself as an ally rather than a conventional salesperson. By expressing eagerness to go the extra mile, you communicate that your interest goes beyond selling a product. You actively seek to contribute to the customer's success and satisfaction, aligning with the modern shift towards more customer-centric sales strategies.

Building a Mutual Relationship:

Creating a mutual relationship mutual relationship is inherent in all successful business interactions. It's not a one-sided exchange; it's about establishing a connection where both parties benefit. Your excitement about what you can do for the customer reflects your commitment to adding value beyond the transaction.

Showing You Are There to Help:

Demonstrating that you are there to help transforms the interaction from a one-time transaction into the beginning of a long-term, mutually beneficial relationship. This goes beyond the immediate sale and positions you as a reliable resource. Your excitement is not solely driven by the prospect of closing a deal but by the genuine desire to assist the customer in achieving their goals.

Conclusion:

In essence, getting REAL and answering the question prompts you to shift from a transactional mindset to a relationship-oriented one. It encourages you to find personal ways to add value, demonstrate commitment, and build trust. The excitement here is not just about the sale; it's about the prospect of forging a meaningful, long-lasting connection. Embrace the opportunity to showcase personalized value and set the stage for a relationship that extends far beyond a single transaction.

Question 5: Do you really know where they are coming from?

Understanding the customer's motives is key. Knowing whether they were directed to you, their goals, or potential challenges they might be facing allows you to tailor your approach. This insight helps in building a more personalized and effective sales strategy.

Elaboration:

In the intricate dance of sales, understanding where the customer is coming from is foundational. This question delves into the motives that drive their engagement, recognizing that their situation significantly influences their needs, expectations, and potential challenges.

Tailoring the Approach:

The response highlights the importance of tailoring your approach based on a deep understanding of the customer's motives. It acknowledges that a one-size-fits-all strategy is insufficient, and effective sales require customization. Knowing whether the customer was directed to you or if they have specific goals provides crucial context for shaping your engagement.

Directed to You by Someone Else:

One potential scenario is whether the customer was asked to reach out by someone else. This could indicate a situation where the customer might not be fully invested in the interaction. They could be following instructions but may not be genuinely interested. Recognizing this possibility allows the salesperson to adapt their approach, perhaps by building rapport more deliberately or addressing any reservations the customer may have.

Personal Goals or Professional Motivations:

Understanding whether the customer is trying to avoid getting fired, aiming for a raise, or using your services for information to purchase elsewhere sheds light on their personal and professional motivations. This insight enables the salesperson to align their pitch with the customer's goals, making the interaction more relevant and appealing.

Potential Challenges:

Acknowledging the potential challenges, the customer might be facing is another critical aspect. Whether it's internal dynamics within their organization or external market pressures, recognizing these challenges allows the salesperson to position their product or service as a solution. It demonstrates empathy and positions the sales conversation as a collaborative effort to overcome obstacles.

Building a Personalized and Effective Sales Strategy:

The core message is clear: understanding where the customer is coming from is essential for building a personalized and effective sales strategy. It's not just about promoting the features of your product or service but about aligning with the customer's unique situation and needs. This approach moves beyond a transactional interaction to a consultative engagement where the salesperson becomes a problem-solver and a valuable partner.

Empathy in Sales:

This question inherently recognizes the importance of empathy in sales. By understanding the customer's motives, challenges, and goals, the salesperson can demonstrate genuine interest and care. This empathetic approach is a powerful tool for building rapport and trust, two foundational elements of successful sales relationships.

Conclusion:

In conclusion, the question "Do you really know where they are coming from?" underscores the significance of understanding the customer's motives. Whether they were directed by someone else, driven by personal goals, or facing specific challenges, this knowledge enables the salesperson to tailor their approach, making the interaction more personalized and effective. It's about moving beyond a transactional mindset and embracing a consultative approach that addresses the unique needs of each customer.

Question 6: Do they know what you are really doing for them?

You need to efficiently communicate all the things you personally are going to do for the customer to make sure they are represented in every aspect of the sales process. It is truly essential for starting to create the separation of you from your company and building a relationship with your customer or client. This chapter delves into the critical aspect of making the customer fully aware of the value-added, transcending the traditional boundaries of products or services to create a strong foundation of a lasting and meaningful relationship.

The Power of Personal Communication:

It is so important to articulate the personal endeavors you are willing to do on behalf of the customer. It's not just about the company's offerings; it's about the unique contributions, the extra mile taken, and the personalized commitment to the customer's satisfaction.

Separation of You from Your Company:

The answer underscores the necessity of creating a clear separation between the you and the company. While the product or service may be the initial point of contact, establishing a personal connection is pivotal. It's about going beyond the corporate identity and showcasing the individual dedication to meeting the customer's needs.

Building a Relationship Beyond Transactions:

Effective communication of personal efforts is the catalyst for building relationships that transcend mere transactions. It marks the beginning of a separation, where the salesperson emerges not just as a representative of the company but as a dedicated ally invested in the customer's journey.

Negotiating Better Terms:

Suppose a customer express's concerns about pricing. Communicating the active efforts to negotiate better terms on their behalf not only highlights your commitment but also provides transparency into the intricacies of pricing negotiations.

Advocating for the Customer:

If discussions with higher-ups are required to tailor a solution to the customer's specific needs, make this known. Advocating for the customer within the company showcases a personalized commitment to ensuring their requirements are not just met but prioritized.

Providing Additional Benefits:

Examples like offering custom solutions, providing exclusive discounts, or ensuring a seamless onboarding process are tangible manifestations of personal efforts. These actions extend beyond the core product or service, adding genuine value to the customer's experience.

Strengthening the Foundation:

The essence here is not only meeting the customer's expectations but surpassing them. Communicating personal efforts creates transparency, establishing a foundation of trust. It transforms the sales journey from a transactional encounter to a collaborative relationship built on mutual understanding and dedication.

Becoming a Trusted Advisor:

By ensuring the customer is fully aware of the efforts made on their behalf, you will be transformed into a trusted advisor. This shift elevates the relationship beyond a mere buyer-seller dynamic to a partnership where both parties actively contribute to each other's success.

In conclusion, the chapter elucidates the paramount importance of efficiently communicating personal efforts in the sales process. It's about more than the product or service; it's about the dedication, advocacy, and personalized commitment to the customer's journey. This transparency lays the groundwork for trust, strengthens the relationship, and positions you not just as a representative of the company but as a reliable partner genuinely invested in the customer's success. It is a fundamental step toward crafting lasting and meaningful connections in the world of sales.

Question 7: Have you told them who's team your on?

You must clearly communicate that you're on the customer's team, playing the role of a consultant committed to their needs, not just representing the company you work for or own.

Elaboration:

A common piece of advice in sales—be a consultant is commonplace. However, be a consultant for whom? Merely being a consultant for the company you work for is insufficient. Instead, the key is to communicate to the customer that you're on their team, playing the role of a consultant committed to their specific needs.

Establishing Yourself as an Ally:

You need to positioning yourself as an ally for the customer. In the traditional sales dynamic, customers might perceive salespeople as representatives of the company's interests. This perspective might create skepticism, as customers question whether the salesperson is genuinely prioritizing their needs. By explicitly stating that you're on their team, you transform the relationship. It becomes a collaborative effort rather than a transactional one.

Mutual Goal Setting:

By committing to be on their team, it shifts the narrative from a seller-buyer relationship to a partnership where both parties share a common objective. By verbalizing your commitment to securing the best deal for the customer, you align your goals with theirs, creating a sense of collaboration.

Playing the Middle:

The notion of playing the middle further emphasizes the commitment to the customer's team. It suggests that you are not merely aligning with the company's goals but actively positioning yourself between the customer and the company. This strategic placement communicates that your loyalty and commitment are with the customer's interests, acting as a bridge between their needs and the offerings of the company.

Commitment to Their Team:

The repeated emphasis on commitment underlines its significance in this context. It's not just about providing a service or selling a product; it's about committing to the customer's goals and needs. This commitment is what differentiates a salesperson from a trusted advisor. By being on their team, you signal that your primary concern is their satisfaction and success.

Being a Consultant to Them, Not the Company:

The distinction made between being a consultant to the customer, not just the company, reinforces the idea of personalized service. It's about understanding the unique needs, challenges, and goals of the customer and tailoring your advice and solutions accordingly. This approach aligns with the evolving expectations of customers who seek personalized and client-centric interactions.

Strengthening Trust:

Trust is a fundamental element in any successful sales relationship. By explicitly stating whose team you're on, you remove ambiguity and assure the customer that your allegiance is with them. This transparency contributes to a more open and honest dynamic, fostering trust and paving the way for a more collaborative and enduring relationship.

Conclusion:

In conclusion, telling the customer whose team you're on is not just a phrase but a strategic move in building a meaningful sales relationship. It communicates commitment, loyalty, and a dedication to serving the customer's unique needs, ultimately creating a bond that goes beyond a simple transaction.

Question 8: Have you acknowledged what they have to offer you?

Beyond recognizing the person you are trying to sell benefits, acknowledging the unique strengths of the individual you're dealing with personalizes the interaction. Complimenting their knowledge or expertise builds rapport and changes the dynamics of the sale.

Elaboration:

Acknowledging what a custom has to offer you introduces a subtle yet powerful shift in perspective. While acknowledging the benefits of the company you're selling to is common practice, acknowledging what the individual person brings to the table adds a layer of personalization and appreciation to the sales dynamic.

Recognizing Personal Contributions:

It's not only about what the company can offer but also about acknowledging what the specific person you're dealing with brings to the interaction. For instance, if you're engaging with a decision-maker in a hospital, acknowledging their role and influence becomes crucial. This could involve recognizing their knowledge, expertise, or their ability to champion the product or service within their organization.

Personalization and Rapport Building:

By going beyond the generic sales pitch and expressing genuine appreciation for the individual's contributions, you personalize the interaction. This personalization is a key factor in building rapport. Complimenting their knowledge or expertise signals that you see them as more than just a conduit to the organization. It creates a connection that goes beyond the transactional nature of the sale.

Changing the Dynamics of the Sale:

Acknowledging what the person has to offer you is not just a nicety; it's a strategic move that can change the entire dynamics of the sale. Most sales interactions focus on what the salesperson can offer to the customer. However, flipping the script and recognizing the value the customer brings to the sales process is a refreshing change. It sets you apart from other salespeople and demonstrates a level of respect and understanding that is often lacking in typical sales engagements.

Boosting Confidence and Trust:

Complimenting the person's knowledge or expertise not only acknowledges their value but also boosts their confidence in the decision-making process. It implies that their input is crucial, creating a sense of empowerment. This boost in confidence can contribute significantly to building trust, as the individual feels seen, appreciated, and understood.

Creating a Lasting Impression:

Acknowledging the person's contributions is a simple yet impactful way to create a lasting impression. In a world where sales interactions can often feel transactional and impersonal, taking the time to recognize the unique strengths of the individual sets a positive tone. It leaves a mark, fostering a sense of goodwill that can extend beyond the immediate sale.

Conclusion:

In conclusion, acknowledging what the person you're dealing with has to offer you is a subtle art in sales. It involves recognizing and complimenting their unique strengths, be it their knowledge, expertise, or influence within their organization. This personalization not only builds rapport but also changes the dynamics of the sale, creating a more collaborative and mutually respectful relationship.

Question 9: Do they trust you?

The question of trust is at the heart of every successful sales relationship. In a world where trust is paramount, understanding whether the customer trusts you is a critical aspect of effective selling. The acknowledgment that not every customer may trust you from the outset is a realistic perspective and it doesn't mean they won't buy from you.

The Importance of Trust:

Trust is the bedrock of any meaningful relationship, and the sales relationship is no exception. While the techniques and approaches taught here are designed to build trust, there will inevitably be instances where trust doesn't come easily. It might be due to past negative experiences, skepticism, or simply a cautious approach on the customer's part.

The Power of the questions above:

All the techniques presented in the questions above can often be very effective in garnering trust. By following the principles discussed—such as recognizing the customer's unique qualities and appreciating what they bring to the interaction—the salesperson positions themselves as more than just someone pushing a product or service. They become a collaborator, a partner in the customer's journey and trust usually comes along with that.

The Role of Past Experiences:

Understanding that past experiences can shape a customer's trust level is crucial. Bad experiences with previous sales interactions can lead to skepticism and wariness. By recognizing this possibility, you can approach the situation with empathy and a commitment to rebuilding trust through positive engagement.

Techniques to Foster Trust:

The techniques taught above, particularly acknowledging what the customer can do for you and expressing appreciation for the customer's knowledge or attributes, is an amazing technique to foster trust. Complimenting the customer's expertise goes beyond the transactional nature of the sale; it communicates genuine respect and recognition of their unique contributions.

Being on Their Team:

The concept of being on the customer's team, as discussed in previous questions, ties into building trust. When the customer senses that the salesperson is genuinely committed to their needs and acknowledges their value, trust naturally begins to form. It's about creating a connection that transcends the immediate transaction and focuses on the long-term relationship.

Building Appreciation:

The idea that these techniques can get customers to appreciate the salesperson as someone on their team reinforces the notion that trust is a two-way street. It's not just about the customer trusting the salesperson; it's also about the salesperson earning the customer's trust by demonstrating a sincere commitment to their success.

Selling to the Untrusting:

While it's undoubtedly easier to sell to someone who trusts you, it's not impossible to sell to someone who doesn't. This is an empowering perspective. It underscores the notion that, even in situations where trust is initially lacking, the right approach and techniques can bridge that gap and pave the way for a mutually beneficial relationship.

Conclusion:

In essence, the question of trust is an important aspect of sales that can be created easily by all the techniques being taught by these questions and answers. You need to recognize its importance, understand the potential influence of past experiences, and leverage techniques that foster trust. Trust, once established, becomes the cornerstone of a successful and enduring sales relationship.

Question 10: What does your product or service do better?

In the world of sales, the question of what makes your product or service superior is a staple. Sales literature often emphasizes the importance of showcasing features and benefits, but the examples provided underscore the value of simplicity in communicating these advantages. The key takeaway is that while it's crucial to highlight what sets your product apart, bombarding the client with overwhelming details can be counterproductive. Instead, the emphasis should be on clear, straightforward advantages communicated in simple language.

Simplicity is Convincing:

Instead of delving into an exhaustive list of features and benefits, my advice is to keep things simple and communicate the key advantages in straightforward terms. When seeking advice from a friend, you wouldn't expect to be bombarded with intricate details but rather receive simple advice. " I feel this one is the best!" or "This is my favorite!"

Avoid Overwhelming Details:

The response underscores the potential pitfalls of getting too specific, using the example of multiple "this" statements. It suggests that beyond a certain point, such specifics can lead to a loss of engagement and make the interaction feel more like a sales pitch. You want to avoid overwhelming the customer with details and instead focus on simplicity.

This aligns with the understanding that a client or customer is more likely to be convinced by a straightforward presentation of key benefits rather than an exhaustive list of features. It's a reminder that the goal is not to showcase every intricate detail but to communicate the standout advantages in a manner that resonates with the customer.

The key phrase "Our product is better because of this" encapsulates the essence of the recommended approach. Rather than delving into an extensive enumeration of features, the suggestion is to use simple language to convey why your product or service is superior. This approach maintains clarity and avoids overwhelming the client.

The emphasis is on clear, straightforward advantages that can be easily understood and appreciated by the customer. By simplifying the message, the goal is to make the case for your product without sounding overly sales-oriented. This approach acknowledges that the modern consumer appreciates authenticity and straightforwardness over intricate sales pitches.

Stand Out Without Sounding Salesy:

In the modern sales landscape, where consumers are inundated with information, standing out is crucial. The response advocates for simplicity as the key to achieving this. By avoiding a salesy approach and opting for clear, straightforward communication of advantages, you can capture the customer's attention without overwhelming them.

Renowned brands like Mercedes, Lexus, and Rolls Royce, don't rely on an exhaustive list of benefits to convince customers. Instead, they confidently assert that their products are better. This showcases the power of simplicity and confidence in asserting superiority.

Conclusion:

In answering the question of what your product or service does better, I want to emphasize the art of simplicity. While it's important to communicate key advantages, the advice is to steer clear of overwhelming details. The goal is to convey superiority in a clear, straightforward manner, steering away from a salesy tone. This approach aligns with the evolving preferences of modern consumers who appreciate authenticity, simplicity, and confidence in product messaging. Ultimately, the power lies in the ability to stand out without bombarding the customer with excessive information.

Question 11: Are you really helping them?

Beyond the product, consider how it personally affects them. Recognize the impact on their life or work, fostering a deeper understanding of the value you bring.

Elaboration:

At the heart of successful sales is a profound understanding that goes beyond the features of your product or service. The question, "Are you really helping them?" reflects the essence of customer-centric sales. It's about acknowledging the individual behind the decision-maker, recognizing their needs, and understanding the personal impact of your offering on their life or work.

Transcending Functional Benefits:

While many sales discussions focus on the functional benefits of a product or service, this question challenges us to consider the emotional and personal implications. It acknowledges that the value proposition extends beyond the product's specifications to how it influences the customer's daily life or professional responsibilities.

Recognizing the Personal Impact:

It is important to recognize the personal impact on the customer's life or work. This acknowledgment is a powerful tool for building a deeper connection. Understanding how your offering affects them on a personal level enables you to tailor your communication and highlight the aspects that resonate most with their individual needs.

Empathy and Understanding:

This question inherently calls for empathy and understanding in the sales process. It requires the salesperson to step into the customer's shoes, acknowledging that every purchase decision, no matter how business-oriented, has personal implications. By demonstrating this understanding, you position yourself not just as a seller but as a partner genuinely invested in the customer's well-being.

Impact on Decision-Making:

Understanding how your product or service affects the customer personally can significantly influence their decision-making process. If they see a direct and positive impact on their life or work, it adds a layer of motivation to the purchase. On the other hand, if the personal implications are not apparent, it raises questions about the genuine value your offering brings to their overall experience.

Value Beyond Transactions:

This question reframes the sales interaction from a transactional perspective to one centered on value. It prompts salespeople to consider the broader significance of their offering in the customer's life. The goal is not just to make a sale but to genuinely enhance the customer's experience and contribute positively to their personal or professional journey.

Tailoring Your Approach:

Understanding the personal impact also allows for a more tailored approach. It enables you to align your communication with the aspects of your product or service that matter most to the customer. If it directly improves their efficiency, reduces stress, or enhances their personal life, these are the points to emphasize.

Building Meaningful Connections:

Ultimately, this question is about building meaningful connections. When customers feel that you genuinely care about how your offering affects them personally, it strengthens the relationship. It positions you as a trusted advisor, someone who is not just selling a product but is actively contributing to the improvement of their life or work.

Incorporating Your Own Insights:

In addition to the concepts outlined, consider incorporating your own insights into the sales process. Personalization is a key element of effective sales, and understanding the unique circumstances and preferences of each customer allows you to tailor your approach more precisely.

Conclusion:

In conclusion, the question "Are you really helping them?" encapsulates the essence of customer-centric sales. It directs our focus beyond the transaction to the personal impact of our offerings on the customer's life or work. Recognizing this impact, demonstrating empathy, and tailoring our approach accordingly are essential steps toward building lasting and meaningful connections in the world of sales.

Question 12: Do they like you?

In the realm of sales, personal likability can play a significant role in building rapport and fostering positive relationships. However, the reality is that not everyone will necessarily like you, and that's perfectly okay. This question, "Do they like you?" prompts a nuanced exploration of the dynamics between a salesperson and a potential customer. Trust and likability are not always connected and knowing the difference is an important aspect in creating a valid selling relationship.

The Importance of Likability:

Personal likability often facilitates smoother interactions and can contribute to building trust. Customers are more likely to engage in open and honest conversations when they feel a positive connection with the salesperson. This likability factor can be influenced by various elements, including shared interests, communication style, and cultural compatibility.

Building Genuine Connections:

It is important to build genuine connections, focusing on shared values or goals that transcend mere likability. While it's natural to desire positive relationships with customers, it's equally crucial to recognize that different personalities may not always align. The emphasis shifts toward authenticity and reliability, foundational elements that can foster a positive connection even in the absence of strong personal liking.

Being on Their Team:

The concept of being on the customer's team, as discussed in previous questions, remains pivotal. Regardless of personal likability, aligning yourself with the customer's goals, committing to their success, and demonstrating genuine interest in helping them create a bond that goes beyond mere friendship. This approach underscores professionalism and dedication to their needs, which can override the personal preference factor.

Commitment to Their Success:

Expressing commitment to the customer's success, beyond personal affability, is a powerful strategy. It communicates a genuine interest in their well-being and ensures that the focus is on providing value and assistance. This commitment becomes a focal point, showcasing a dedication that extends beyond the realm of personal likability.

Different Personalities, Different Preferences:

Understanding that different personalities may not always align is crucial. People have varied preferences, communication styles, and ways of forming connections. Recognizing this diversity allows you to approach interactions with an open mind, adapting your communication style to cater to the unique needs of each customer.

The Role of Authenticity:

Authenticity is an important catalyst for likability. While personal likability might be subjective and influenced by various factors, being authentic is a universal quality that resonates with people. Customers appreciate genuine interactions, even if the connection doesn't extend to a personal liking. Authenticity builds trust and credibility, creating a foundation for a successful sales relationship.

Navigating Differences:

In sales, the ability to navigate differences in personality or preferences is a valuable skill. Not every interaction will be characterized by personal warmth, but by staying true to your commitment to help and providing reliable service, you can still make a positive impact. Understanding and respecting the diversity of personalities ensures a more inclusive and adaptable approach to sales.

Conclusion:

In conclusion, the question "Do they like you?" is an important step in understanding the nature of interpersonal connections in sales. While likability is a desirable trait, the emphasis here is on building genuine connections, being on the customer's team, and expressing unwavering commitment to their success. This approach acknowledges the diversity of personalities and highlights the importance of authenticity and reliability in fostering positive and lasting relationships in the realm of sales.

Question 13: Have you told them who else you have helped?

You need to share specific examples of how you've helped similar individuals or businesses. This approach is way more effective than just listing clients, showcasing real-world impact.

For instance, instead of stating, "I've worked with several hotels," you might share a story about how you helped a struggling hotel increase bookings by 30% within three months through targeted marketing strategies.

Connecting on a Personal Level:

You need to move beyond a detached client list and establish a personal connection with the prospect. By sharing stories of how you've assisted individuals or businesses facing challenges similar to theirs, you demonstrate an understanding of their specific needs and present yourself as a valuable partner in overcoming obstacles.

Tailoring the Narrative to the Prospect:

The examples provided should resonate with the prospect's industry, challenges, or goals. If your prospect is a tech startup dealing with scalability issues, a relevant example could be how you supported a similar startup in streamlining operations and achieving rapid growth. This tailored approach reinforces your relevance to their unique situation.

Building Trust Through Transparency:

The question encourages transparency and authenticity. Instead of relying on the prestige of client names, the focus is on transparently sharing your experiences in a way that resonates with the prospect. This honesty contributes to building trust, an essential element in any successful business relationship.

Quantifying Success:

Incorporating quantifiable results into your examples adds another layer of impact. If you've helped a client increase revenue, reduce costs, or improve efficiency, providing specific numbers adds credibility. For instance, stating that you helped a business cut operational costs by 20% showcases measurable success.

Conclusion:

In conclusion, You need to move beyond surface-level client name-dropping and delve into meaningful examples of how they've positively impacted similar individuals or businesses. This approach, enriched with relatable stories, personal connections, and quantifiable results, transforms the sales pitch into a compelling narrative. It's about showcasing real-world successes and building trust through transparent communication, ultimately increasing the effectiveness of your sales strategy.

Question 14: Do you deserve their business?

It is time to get REAL and evaluate if you've gone above and beyond in your efforts to earn the business. If you've used all the techniques above to demonstrated commitment, honesty, and provided the best possible solutions, you deserve their business! Confidence in your efforts ensures a more confident sales approach to finishing the sale.

Elaboration:

The question, "Do you deserve their business?" brings the focus back to self-reflection and the efforts made to secure a customer's trust and commitment. It prompts a contemplative assessment of whether you've genuinely earned the right to their business. The answer lies not just in the transactional exchange but in the comprehensive approach to building a relationship.

Confidence through Genuine Efforts:

The response emphasizes that confidence in deserving their business is rooted in the genuine efforts made. It's not just about the product or service you're offering; it's about going above and beyond expectations. Have you bent over backwards to meet their needs? Have you provided great pricing and extra benefits? These are the markers that should instill confidence in your deserving their business.

Reflecting on Your Efforts:

The question encourages a reflective stance, prompting sales professionals to evaluate whether they've truly given their best. It goes beyond the checklist of tasks and delves into the depth of the relationship. Being on their side, offering truthful and transparent communication, and ensuring you've explored every avenue to meet their requirements contribute to the foundation of deserving their business.

Demonstrating Commitment:

The concept of commitment resurfaces here. If you've demonstrated unwavering commitment to understanding and fulfilling the customer's needs, you build a strong case for deserving their business. This commitment is not just about the immediate sale; it extends to the long-term relationship and the value you bring to their business.

Honesty is Huge:

Honesty is a crucial element. If you've been totally truthful in your interactions, it forms a cornerstone of deserving their business. Honesty builds trust, and a trusting relationship is more likely to result in a successful and sustained business partnership.

Learning from Every Interaction:

There might be instances where you feel you don't deserve the business. However, it is an opportunity for learning and improvement. If you haven't done all that you could for a particular customer, it becomes a lesson for the future. The emphasis is on continuous growth and refining your approach based on experiences.

Confidence as a Sales Asset:

Confidence in deserving their business is not arrogance but a recognition of your efforts and dedication. This confidence becomes an asset in sales interactions. When you genuinely believe in the value you bring and the commitment you've shown, it permeates through your communication and influences the customer's perception positively.

Building Lasting Relationships:

Ultimately, the question transcends the immediate transaction and underscores the importance of building lasting relationships. Confidence in deserving their business is a byproduct of a holistic, customer-centric approach that extends beyond the initial sale. It's about fostering trust, transparency, and a genuine commitment to their success.

Conclusion:

In conclusion, "Do you deserve their business?" is a call for self-reflection and a holistic evaluation of your efforts. Confidence in deserving their business is rooted in the genuine commitment, honesty, and value you bring to the relationship. This question encourages a continuous learning mindset, emphasizing the importance of every interaction in shaping your approach for future engagements.

Question 15: Did they hire you?

Securing the mental commitment from the customer is the ultimate goal! By answering the questions honestly and aligning yourself with their needs, you position yourself as a consultant they've "hired," signaling the completion of the sales process and the beginning of a lasting partnership. This can happen in as little as 10 min if you "Don't Shut the F$CK Up!" and you follow all the steps above. Once they have mentally hired you the sale is done and the rest is making sure you take care of all the details. It is the pinnacle of all the mental preparation created by the questions above!

The Culmination of the Sales Process:

The question, "Did they hire you?" represents the culmination of all the efforts and insights gained from the preceding questions. It's the point where the customer mentally commits to you, recognizing your value beyond a mere sales transaction. This mental hiring signifies that you've successfully navigated the intricacies of the sales relationship and positioned yourself as a consultant.

The Mental Shift:

Getting hired in this context is not about signing a contract; it's a mental shift in the customer's perception. It goes beyond a simple purchase decision. It represents the customer acknowledging that you are not just a salesperson but someone they trust, value, and consider as a consultant. This shift is a game-changer, signaling a move from transactional to relational.

Alignment with Customer Needs:

To secure this mental commitment, it's crucial to align yourself with the customer's needs and concerns throughout the sales process. This involves addressing questions about the product's relevance, the benefits it brings, and what the customer offers your company. By being genuine and transparent, you build trust and credibility, paving the way for this mental hiring to take place.

Consultant Relationship:

Being "hired" as a consultant means that the customer views you as more than just a seller. They recognize your expertise and commitment to their needs. This relationship is based on mutual respect, understanding, and a shared goal of achieving the best possible outcome. Once you've attained this consultant status, the focus shifts from convincing to collaborating.

Fine-Tuning the Details:

After being mentally hired, the sales process is essentially won. The subsequent steps involve fine-tuning the details and addressing any specific requirements or concerns the customer may have. This could include finalizing the terms, clarifying delivery logistics, or customizing the solution further based on their preferences. The emphasis is on ensuring a smooth transition from the mental commitment to the practical implementation of the sale.

Unique Examples:

Consider a scenario where a customer, after thorough discussions about the product's features and benefits, acknowledges that your solution perfectly aligns with their needs. They express their confidence in your expertise and commitment to addressing their specific requirements, signaling the mental hiring process.

In a B2B setting, your ability to understand and appreciate the unique value the customer brings to your company could be the deciding factor. If you convey genuine excitement about working with them, recognizing their individuality and what they offer your business, it strengthens the customer's perception of your commitment.

Imagine a situation where, during the sales process, you acknowledge the challenges the customer might face in implementing the product. By proactively providing solutions and showcasing your dedication to their success, you build the trust needed for them to mentally hire you as their consultant.

Conclusion:

"Did they hire you?" marks the pinnacle of the sales journey. It's the point where the customer mentally commits to your expertise and values the relationship beyond a transaction. This question encapsulates the essence of effective sales – building trust, understanding needs, and positioning yourself as a valuable consultant. Once mentally hired, the focus shifts to refining the details, solidifying the partnership, and ensuring a successful and lasting relationship.

www.ingramcontent.com/pod-product-compliance
Lightning Source LLC
Chambersburg PA
CBHW071004290526
45795CB00005B/1766